Traveling Around Alaska

by Lillian Rose

illustrated by Leslie Evans

Contents

Introduction 3
Brief History 4
The Alaska Highway 6
The Effects of Change 9
Alaska Now 11
Glossary 16

Harcourt

Orlando Boston Dallas Chicago San Diego

Visit *The Learning Site!*
www.harcourtschool.com

ALASKA

Nome

Fairbanks

CANADA

Yukon Territory

Alaska Highway

Anchorage

Seward

Juneau

Aleutian Islands

Pacific Ocean

2

On-Level Book
Grade 5

5 copies of
Traveling Around Alaska

Harcourt

Orlando Boston Dallas Chicago San Diego

Visit *The Learning Site!*
www.harcourtschool.com

Copyright © by Harcourt, Inc.
All rights reserved.
ISBN 0-15-327419-0

3 4 5 6 7 8 9 10   126   10 09 08 07 06 05 04

0-15-327419-0

flysheet 9997-36371-X

Introduction

What do you think of when you hear the word *Alaska*? Perhaps you picture a vast wilderness of snow and ice. To travel in such a place would be difficult. The only way you can imagine anyone could travel from place to place is by dogsled.

Your picture would be only partly correct. Alaska makes up one-sixth of the area of the United States. Spread out over that vast space is one of the smallest populations in the country. Of course, there is snow much of the year. Yet today there are many ways to travel around Alaska, and traveling by dogsled is just one of them.

Brief History

To understand what Alaska is like now, it is helpful to know some of its history. The United States bought Alaska from Russia in 1867. William H. Seward was Secretary of State at the time. Some Americans thought he had bought a worthless wilderness of ice and snow. They called it Seward's Folly, Seward's Icebox, and even Icebergia. Yet buying the Alaskan frontier turned out to be a very wise decision. Alaska is rich in fish, minerals, timber, oil, and other resources.

BLOCKADE OF PACKERS WHITE PASS TRAIL

As more people went to Alaska to claim those resources, the need for reliable transportation increased. This became especially clear after the discovery of gold in Nome in 1899. Thousands of people rushed to Alaska, hoping to get rich. In ten years, the territory's population nearly doubled. Something had to be done by the U.S. government to make travel to and across Alaska easier.

In the early 1900s Congress created a system of wagon roads, trails, and bridges in Alaska. Ferries began to carry goods and passengers along Alaska's long coastline. In 1923, the Alaska Railroad was built, connecting Seward with Anchorage and Fairbanks.

The Alaska Highway

Probably no event changed transportation in Alaska as much as World War II. The war was fought in both Europe and Asia. The U.S. government realized that Alaska might become the target of an invasion by the Japanese Army. If you look at a globe from above, centered on the Arctic Ocean, you can see why. Alaska is the point in North America that is closest to Asia. In fact, some of the Aleutian Islands, off the coast of Alaska, were the only part of North America to be invaded during the war.

The U.S. government decided to set up military positions in Alaska. However, sending thousands of soldiers to Alaska meant that an emergency overland supply route was needed. The U.S. Army Corps of Engineers developed a plan for a highway that was 1,523 miles [2,451 km] long, and then built it in eight months in 1942. Construction included airports, side roads, and headquarters at military bases. The men worked at a fast pace, despite such problems as below-freezing temperatures, blizzards, and mud. This engineering marvel was built by more than 11,000 American troops, many of whom were engineers, and 16,000 civilian workers from the United States and Canada.

7

Map showing the Alaska Highway running from Dawson Creek through the Yukon Territory to Fairbanks, Alaska.

The total cost of building the Alaska Highway was $135 million. The road has become one of the most important transportation routes in North America, connecting Dawson Creek in British Columbia, Canada, to Fairbanks, Alaska. The road goes through the Yukon Territory. The Alaska Highway has been called many names, which reflect its various uses: the Alcan, or Alaska-Canadian Highway, the Alaska International Highway, and the Alaska Military Highway.

The Effects of Change

The highway brought many changes to the land. It also affected those who live on the land, especially native peoples such as the Inuit and Aleut. The traditional life of the Inuit (also called Eskimo) was well adapted to a cold, snow-covered world. The Inuit traveled the miles of natural waterways in skin-covered one-person boats called *kayaks* and larger boats called *umiaks*. On land they used dogsleds to travel through the frozen landscape. Traditionally, the Aleut traveled in one- and two-person skin boats named *bidarkas*. The first European explorers and traders brought changes to the lives of these native peoples, but nothing compared to the changes caused by the Alaska Highway.

Picture a pair of mushers in the 1940s coming back from a trading post, headed to their camp. Their dogsleds are piled high with goods that will keep them fed and warm for several months. Then, without warning, they come across a path that has just been cut through the snow. The handlers stop their sleds so suddenly that the lines tangle. They can only sit and stare as a huge earth-moving machine widens the road even more.

Often change was just that quick, with the old giving way almost instantaneously to the new. For many native-born Alaskans, their way of life had varied little over the years. Hunting, fishing, and trading were how they earned their living. Imagine how they must have felt about the sudden changes the new roads brought. The changes were, of course, especially dramatic for those living in the remotest areas that the Alaska Highway and its connecting roads touched.

The new roads also brought many more people to Alaska, including members of the armed forces and various government workers. They came from what Alaskans call the "lower forty-eight," the states that lie south of the Canadian border. That trend would continue, as more and more of the population of Alaska came to be made up of people who had been born elsewhere. Most of these people followed more modern ways of life. Native-born Alaskans—of Aleut, Inuit, Native American, and European descent—understood that their old way of life was surely going to change.

Alaska Now

Despite the changes, much that is traditional has remained the same. In 1959 Alaska became the forty-ninth state. Juneau is the capital, but Anchorage is the only major city in terms of population. More than half of all Alaskans live in the Greater Anchorage area. Most of the remainder live around Fairbanks or in the southern panhandle. Small groups of people are scattered in villages on the Arctic plains and Aleutian Islands. The population of Nome—where the gold rush began over one hundred years ago—has decreased dramatically since 1900, when 20,000 gold miners stampeded there. In 1990 Nome had only 3,500 residents.

Part of Alaska's population has always lived in the vast wilderness. Many of these people lead lives much the same as those of their grandparents. They log, mine, hunt, and fish. Sled dogs are still a part of life in Alaska, though more Inuit are choosing snowmobiles for travel across the snow. City residents appreciate that the wilderness is only a few miles, even minutes, away. It's one reason that Alaska is known as the last American frontier.

That feeling of being so close to the wilderness is what makes Alaska such a popular attraction for visitors who love the outdoors. Many tourists fly into the state, and others arrive there on ships and in cars, buses, and recreational vehicles. Vacationers from the lower forty-eight now travel the Alaska Highway that was built to carry military supplies. They can also turn off onto local roads to explore less-traveled paths. If they wish, vacationers can keep heading north and drive beyond the Arctic Circle, almost to the Arctic Ocean! Once in Alaska, some tourists fly in small bush planes or seaplanes to the parts of Alaska where there are still no roads. Tourists can even take helicopter trips to view panoramas of glaciers and ice fields.

During the 1960s, the new state worked on improving its transportation facilities. The Alaska Marine Highway is the ferry system the state designed to serve its coastal cities. Thousands of residents and tourists use this vast system of 500-passenger, 100-car ferries. Other visitors sail along the Alaska coast aboard huge cruise ships that are floating luxury hotels. Smaller cruise ships also take tourists past centuries-old glaciers. Then there are the modern kayaks that dot the water, allowing people to explore Alaska's 15,000 square miles of fjords and other inlets and 34,000 miles of tidal coastline.

No matter what way visitors arrive, Alaska has a special attraction for people who are seeking wilderness experiences. Climbers like the challenge of the Alaska Range, whose mountains are the highest in North America. In fact, the sixteen highest mountains in the United States are found in Alaska. Campers come to hike and backpack the thousands of trails that provide access to beautiful rivers, lakes, and streams. Other visitors come to take photographs, to fish, to raft down rivers, to ride bikes and horses, to ski, to try dogsledding, or to snowmobile.

Along the way visitors have the chance to meet the people of Alaska. In some places, though, especially where there are fewer humans, they might encounter other residents of Alaska traveling by land, sea, or air. Alaska has many types of wildlife, some of which you don't find in the lower forty-eight.

Animals Native to Alaska

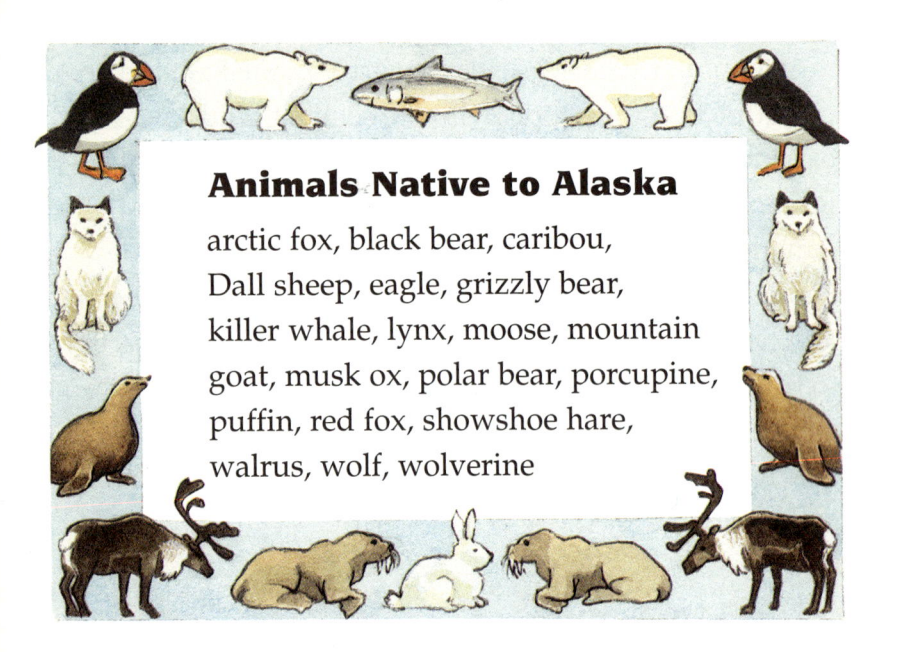

arctic fox, black bear, caribou, Dall sheep, eagle, grizzly bear, killer whale, lynx, moose, mountain goat, musk ox, polar bear, porcupine, puffin, red fox, showshoe hare, walrus, wolf, wolverine

Glossary

bush wilderness part of Alaska that is nearly impossible to get to by car
civilian not part of the military
descent origins, heritage
ferries boats that ferry (carry) people and vehicles
folly foolishness
frontier area beyond settlements
glacier large body of slow-moving ice
instantaneously in a way that happens in a second
marine involving the sea
panhandle part of southwestern Alaska shaped like a handle on a pan
remote very far off
vast huge